W9-AZT-977

THE STORY OF ME AND MY
GRANDPA

First published by Parragon Books Ltd in 2013
LIFE CANVAS is an imprint of Parragon Books Ltd

Parragon
Chartist House
15-17 Trim Street
Bath BA1 1HA, UK
www.parragon.com

Copyright © Parragon Books Ltd 2013

LIFE CANVAS and the accompanying logo are trademarks of Parragon
Books Ltd

Produced by Tall Tree Ltd
Illustrations by Apple Agency

All rights reserved. No part of this publication may be reproduced,
stored in a retrieval system or transmitted, in any form or by any means,
electronic, mechanical, photocopying, recording or otherwise, without the
prior permission of the copyright holder.

ISBN 978-1-4723-0745-3
GTIN 5060292801056

Printed in China

THIS LITTLE BOOK IS JUST FOR YOU, GRANDPA, BECAUSE...

love from..

where ....

when ....

I LOVE YOU
GRANDPA!

OUR JOURNEY TOGETHER

FOLLOW THIS THREAD
THROUGH THE BOOK TO
SEE PHOTOS THAT MAKE UP
THE STORY OF OUR LIVES
SO FAR AND SHOW SOME
OF THE THINGS WE'VE
DONE TOGETHER.

stick your photo here

GRANDPA
WISHES HE...

Drove this car ....

Looked like ....

Played baseball like ....

Lived in ....

Had time to ....

Worked at ....

Could go on vacation to ....

Had invented ....

Had written ....

Had painted ....

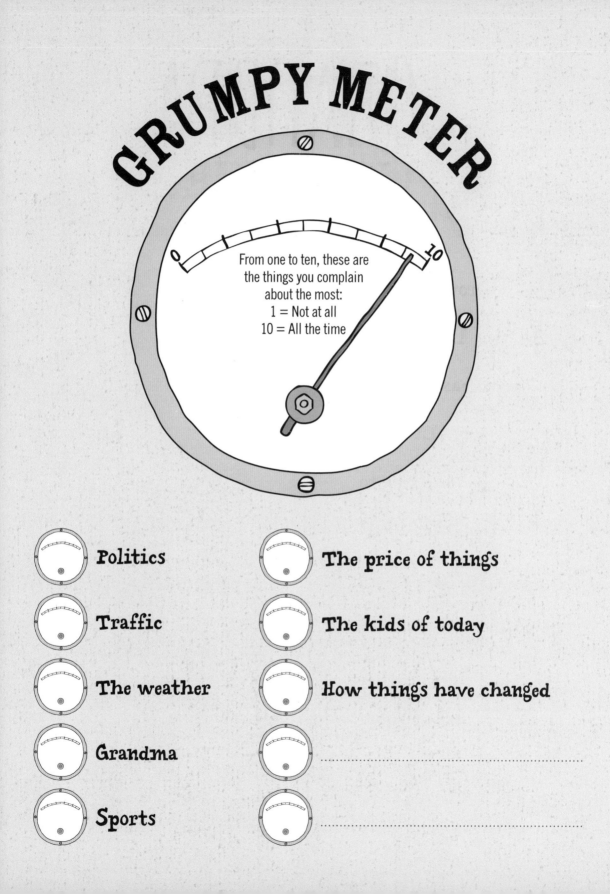

GRUMPY METER

From one to ten, these are the things you complain about the most:
1 = Not at all
10 = All the time

0   10

Politics

Traffic

The weather

Grandma

Sports

The price of things

The kids of today

How things have changed

....

....

GRANDPA AND I HAVE LOTS OF FUN,

....
....
....
....
....
....
....
....
....
....
....
....

BUT THIS TIME WAS THE BEST!

Does Grandpa like doing these things?

	really likes	likes	sort of likes	dislikes
Watching TV	☐	☐	☐	☐
Going to work	☐	☐	☐	☐
Watching his grandchildren	☐	☐	☐	☐
Playing sports	☐	☐	☐	☐
Cooking	☐	☐	☐	☐
Fixing things	☐	☐	☐	☐
Exercising	☐	☐	☐	☐
Shopping for clothes	☐	☐	☐	☐
Shopping for food	☐	☐	☐	☐
Drinking beer	☐	☐	☐	☐
Meeting his friends	☐	☐	☐	☐
Telling jokes	☐	☐	☐	☐
Telling stories	☐	☐	☐	☐
Gardening	☐	☐	☐	☐
....	☐	☐	☐	☐
....	☐	☐	☐	☐
....	☐	☐	☐	☐
....	☐	☐	☐	☐

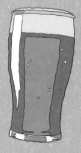

Whenever something goes wrong
GRANDPA SAYS,

and when things go right he says

stick your photo here

THANK YOU GRANDPA

FOR TEACHING ME

1. ....
2. ....
3. ....
4. ....
5. ....
6. ....
7. ....
8. ....
9. ....
10. ....

stick your photo here

If I had a time machine, I would take us back to the time...

....

....

....

....

....

....

....

....

you

me

THIS IS OUR
FAMILY TREE
Fill in the blanks with your grandparents and
parents to make your family tree.

GRANDPA always has THESE THINGS READY TO USE

✓

Screwdriver ☐
Tape measure ☐
Candy ☐
Money ☐
Glasses ☐
Pen ☐
Laptop ☐
Radio ☐
Car keys ☐
Phone ☐

.... ☐
.... ☐
.... ☐

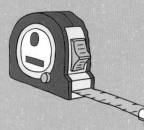

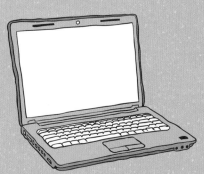

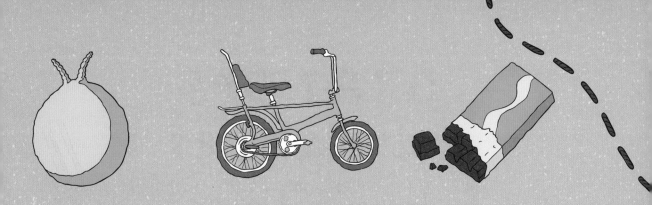

....
....
....
....
....
....
....
....
....
....
....
....
....
....
....
....
....

WHEN GRANDPA WAS LITTLE, HE...

LIKES AND DISLIKES

Grandpa likes to wear ....

Grandpa likes to read ....

Grandpa likes to watch ....

Grandpa likes to play ....

Grandpa likes to eat ....

....

....

Grandpa hates to wear ....

Grandpa hates to read ....

Grandpa hates to watch ....

Grandpa hates to play ....

Grandpa hates to eat ....

....

....

MY FAVORITE
THINGS TO DO WITH YOU

When it's sunny

1. ....
2. ....
3. ....
4. ....
5. ....

When it's raining

1.
2.
3.
4.
5.

When it's cold

1. ....
2. ....
3. ....
4. ....
5. ....

GRANDPA
LOVES TO USE

GRANDPA'S GADGET RATING

Remote controls :(:| :)

Games console :(:| :)

Microwave :(:| :)

Power drill :(:| :)

Smartphone :(:| :)

iPad/Tablet :(:| :)

Computer :(:| :)

MP3 player :(:| :)

E-reader :(:| :)

.... :(:| :)

.... :(:| :)

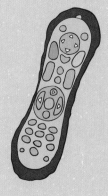
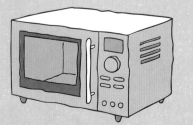

Spot the similarities

Stick in photos and list the similarities.

ME

YOU

MOM/ DAD

GRANDPA
would rate his food

Fried chicken
☆☆☆☆☆

Sandwiches
☆☆☆☆☆

Apple pie
☆☆☆☆☆

Hamburger
☆☆☆☆☆

Spaghetti and meatballs
☆☆☆☆☆

Chocolate brownies
☆☆☆☆☆

Meatloaf
☆☆☆☆☆

Ice cream
☆☆☆☆☆

Pizza
☆☆☆☆☆

GRANDPA'S
BEST
JOKES

···································
···································
···································
···································
···································
···································

···································
···································
···································
···································
···································
···································

GRANDPA'S
WORST
JOKES

stick your photo here

THIS WAS WHEN...

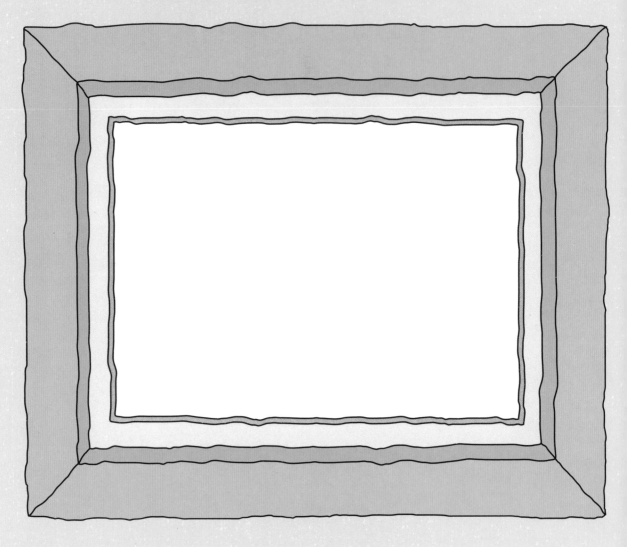

....
....
....
....
....

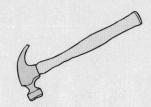

THINGS YOU'VE
FIXED

OR MADE
FOR ME...

....
....
....
....
....
....
....
....

ON A SCALE OF 88 TO 88 YOU'D SCORE

Color in the digital numbers to give your score.

88 **STYLE**

88 **TASTE IN MUSIC**

88 **SPORTS TRIVIA**

88 **KEEPING UP WITH ME**

88 **CHANNEL SURFING**

88 **SENSE OF DIRECTION**

88 **MOVIE TRIVIA**

88 **KNOWING THE WORDS TO SONGS**

88 **KNOWING WHO'S WHO**

88 **SURFING THE INTERNET**

stick your photo here

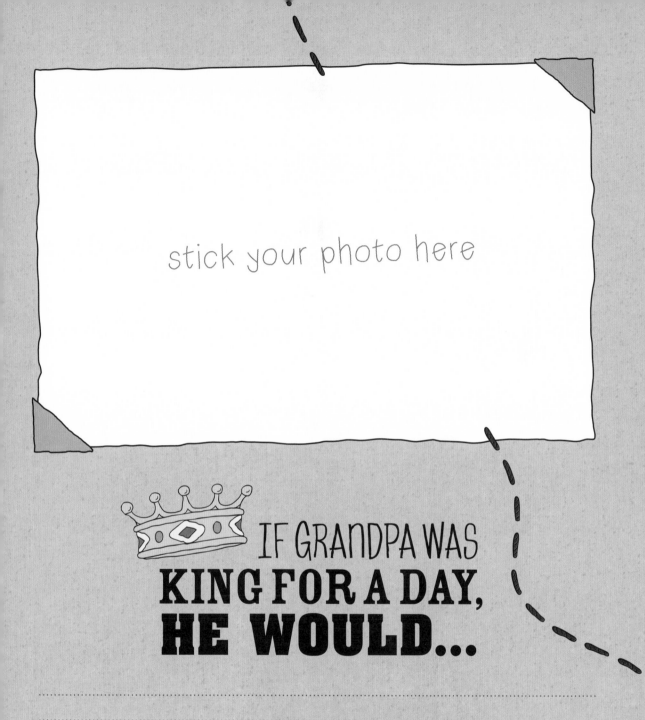

IF GRANDPA WAS
KING FOR A DAY,
HE WOULD...

....

....

....

....

....

GRANDPA'S
FAVORITE CELEBRITIES

1. ....
2. ....
3. ....
4. ....
5. ....

MY
FAVORITE CELEBRITIES

1. ....
2. ....
3. ....
4. ....
5. ....

Kind

Generous

Smart

Strong

Funny

Cranky

A PIZZA OF YOUR PERSONALITY!

Happy

Creative

Brave

Helpful

Look at these words and think of Grandpa and what he's like. Then divide the pizza into the different characteristics that make up his personality.

1. ....
2. ....
3. ....
4. ....
5. ....

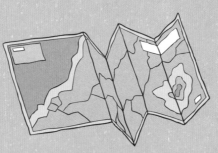

PLACES
GRANDPA AND I
LOVE TO VISIT
TOGETHER

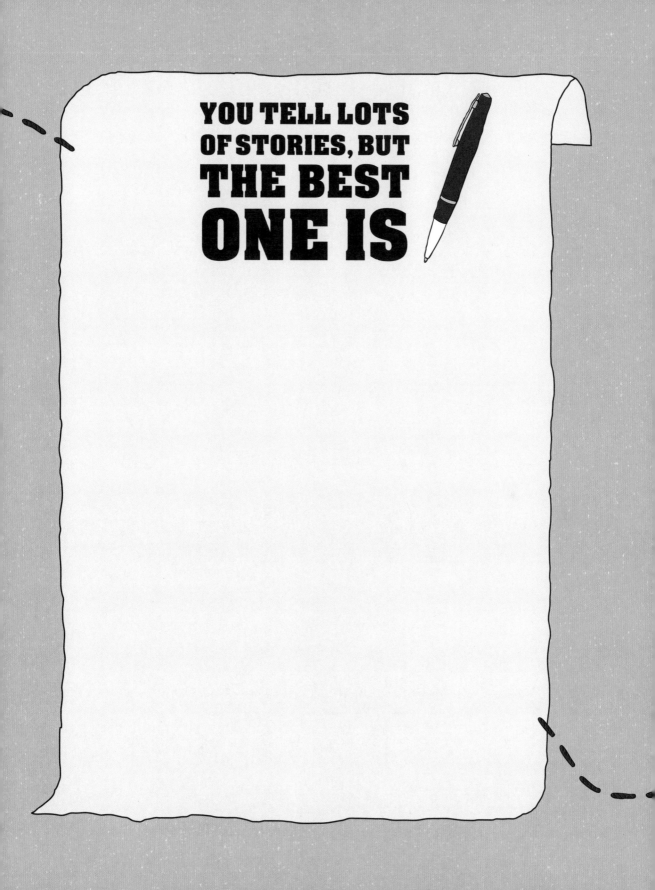

YOU TELL LOTS OF STORIES, BUT **THE BEST ONE IS**

IF I COULD
DO ANYTHING
WITH YOU, I'D...

Morning

....
....
....
....
....
....
....
....
....

Afternoon

....
....
....
....
....

Night

....
....
....
....
....
....
....
....
....
....

stick your photo here

YOU ALWAYS SAY THAT THEY DON'T MAKE THESE THINGS LIKE THEY USED TO

1. ....

2. ....

3. ....

4. ....

5. ....

6. ....

7. ....

I WISH I'D TAKEN A
PHOTO WHEN

GRUMPY GRAPH

Complete this line graph to see how much Grandpa moans.

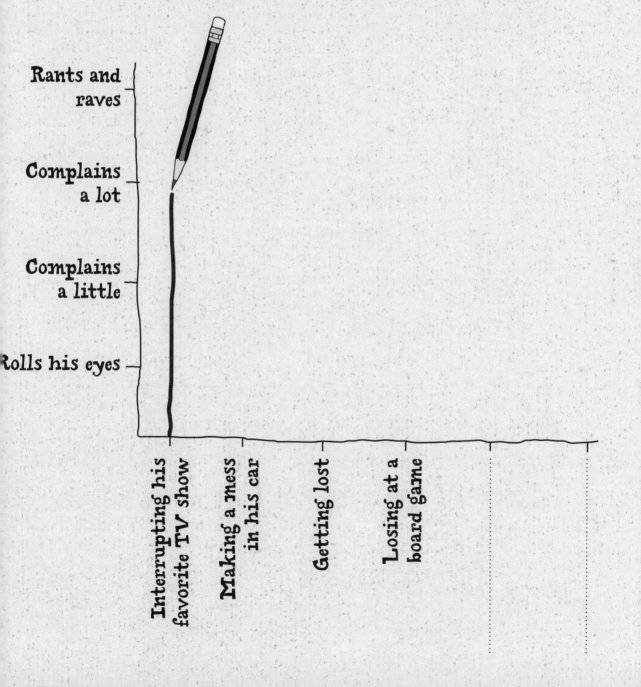

THE CAMERA
NEVER LIES

...GRANDPA CAUGHT ON FILM!

If Grandpa was filling a time capsule now, he would put in...

1. ....
2. ....
3. ....
4. ....
5. ....

1. ....
2. ....
3. ....
4. ....
5. ....

If I was filling a time capsule now, I would put in...

RATING GRANDPA'S SKILLS

Give Grandpa a score from one to ten to see how good he is at...

◯ Fixing things   ◯ Listening

◯ Singing   ◯ Running

◯ Dancing   ◯ Playing games

◯ Cleaning   ◯ ....

◯ Driving   ◯ ....

◯ Cooking   ◯ ....

◯ Storytelling   ◯ ....

We almost got into
TROUBLE WHEN WE...

....

....

....

....

....

....

....

stick your photo here

GRANDPA

spends his time	would like to spend his time	
☐	☐	Reading
☐	☐	Working
☐	☐	In the backyard
☐	☐	Cooking
☐	☐	Cleaning
☐	☐	Playing sports
☐	☐	Fixing things
☐	☐	Watching sports
☐	☐	Doing crossword puzzles
☐	☐	At dinner with his friends
☐	☐	....
☐	☐	....
☐	☐	....
☐	☐	....

GRANDPA SPENDS HIS TIME...

PEOPLE SAY WE HAVE THESE THINGS IN COMMON

1. ....
2. ....
3. ....
4. ....
5. ....

stick your photo here

stick your photo here

I wish these things
FOR YOU

....

....

....

....

....

....

....

....

I ADMIRE YOU BECAUSE...

I LOVE DOING
THESE THINGS WITH
WITH YOU

1. ....

2. ....

3. ....

4. ....

5. ....

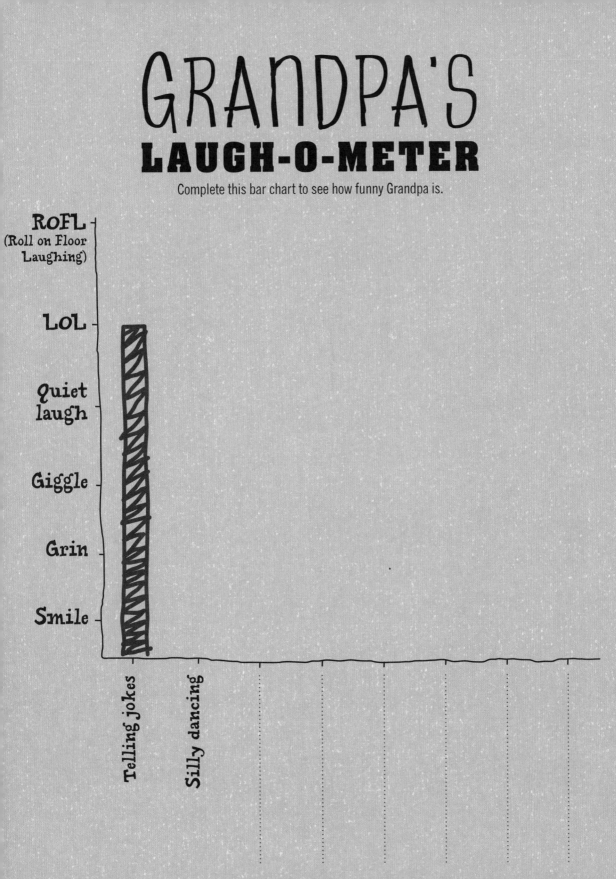

GRANDPA'S
LAUGH-O-METER

Complete this bar chart to see how funny Grandpa is.

RoFL
(Roll on Floor
Laughing)

LoL

Quiet
laugh

Giggle

Grin

Smile

Telling jokes

Silly dancing

WE SHOULD DO THESE THINGS TOGETHER

....
....
....
....
....
....
....
....
....
....
....
....
....
....

WHY YOU MEAN THE WORLD TO ME

THIS IS US NOW

NUMBER 1 GRANDPA

I LOVE YOU GRANDPA!

Best Grandpa

SUPER-GRANDPA

YOU'RE THE BEST!

WORD'S NICEST GRANDPA

World's best Grandpa

Fixed by Grandpa

Time for a treat

Let's go for a walk

Let's go for a ride

Fixed by Grandpa

Time for a treat

Let's go for a walk

Let's go for a ride